Divine Love

Stephen Shaw

Divine Love

ISBN: 978-0-9955928-1-0

Stephen Shaw's Books

Visit the website: www.i-am-stephen-shaw.com

I Am contains spiritual and mystical teachings from enlightened masters that point the way to love, peace, bliss, freedom and spiritual awakening.

Heart Song takes you on a mystical adventure into creating your reality and manifesting your dreams, and reveals the secrets to attaining a fulfilled and joyful life.

They Walk Among Us is a love story spanning two realities. Explore the mystery of the angels. Discover the secrets of Love Whispering.

The Other Side explores the most fundamental question in each reality. What happens when the physical body dies? Where do you go? Expand your awareness. Journey deep into the Mystery.

Reflections offers mystical words for guidance, meditation and contemplation. Open the book anywhere and unwrap your daily inspiration.

5D is the Fifth Dimension. Discover ethereal doorways hidden in the fabric of space-time. Seek the advanced mystical teachings.

Star Child offers an exciting glimpse into the future on earth. The return of the gods and the advanced mystical teachings. And the ultimate battle of light versus darkness.

The Tribe expounds the joyful creation of new Earth. What happened after the legendary battle of Machu Picchu? What is Christ consciousness? What is Ecstatic Tantra?

The Fractal Key reveals the secrets of the shamans. This handbook for psychonauts discloses the techniques and practices used in psychedelic healing and transcendent journeys.

Stephen Shaw's Books

Atlantis illuminates the Star Beings and Earth's Ancient History. A magical history ingrained in your deepest consciousness, in your myths and mysteries. Discover the secret teachings of the star beings.

The Sorcerer is a journey into Magick, Power and Mysticism. Discover the Twelve Auspicious Symbols. Explore the paths of Awareness, Love and Tantra. Absorb the sacred teachings and mantras of the lamas.

Divine Love is a guide on how to truly live. It's about authenticity, intimacy and freedom. It's about discovering and accepting your true nature. Bringing profound, overwhelming Love into your precious existence. Embracing OMGorgeous exquisilicious feelings of fulfilment, peace and joy. Creating a slice of heaven on Earth.

DIVINE LOVERS feel fulfilled and joyful most of the time.

Sometimes they feel ecstatic and fabulous.

Sometimes they just feel good.

Occasionally they cry too.

Feeling good is what drives all our behaviours.

It's why we live; it's why we strive.

Stephen Shaw

BODY

DIVINE LOVERS

embrace

NUTRITION and HEALTH

and let go

DIS-EASE

Your physical body is the *foundation* for feeling good.

If you're not feeling good, always come back to the body.

Are you adopting optimal nutrition that suits your body?

Do you understand the crucial significance of your gut microbiome as primary producer of the 'happiness neurotransmitter' serotonin? And its vital role in overall physical health, optimal immune system, neurogenesis, nutrient absorption, increased vitality and reduced inflammation?

Do you understand the importance of prebiotics, probiotics, polyphenols, fibre and ghee?

Have you had a comprehensive nutritional and food sensitivities test?

Have you had a heavy metals and toxins test?

Have you had a gut microbiome analysis?

Right now, order these excellent books:

Fat For Fuel by Dr Joseph Mercola
Brain Maker by Dr David Perlmutter
The Bulletproof Diet by Dave Asprey
Effortless Healing by Dr Joseph Mercola
The Plant Paradox by Dr Steven Gundry
The Complete Guide To Fasting by Dr Jason Fung

Nutrition is a personal choice. Always do your research, heed medical guidelines, possibly hire the services of a nutritionist, and discover what works best for your body.

MIND

Stephen Shaw

DIVINE LOVERS

embrace

YOU ARE A BOUQUET OF QUALITIES

and let go

RIGID IDENTITY

Gaze at a nearby chair.

Imagine removing the size and shape of the chair.
Imagine removing the colours and patterns.
Imagine removing the texture of the chair.
Imagine removing the scent.

When all its *qualities* are removed, what is left?

Pure, underlying, ubiquitous energy.

The same universal energy underlying everything.

Now, think about YOU.

You are a bit more complex than a chair.

You have many physical, psychological and emotional qualities.

Who are YOU beneath and beyond all your external qualities?

If we are all the same underlying, eternal, permanent, universal energy, why do we hold so strongly onto external, transient, impermanent, ever-changing qualities?

Why do you create an IDENTITY out of transient, impermanent qualities?

Does it help or hinder to rigidly hold onto beliefs and identity?

Is it more useful to be adaptable, flexible and flowing?

All your qualities arise from NATURE and NURTURE and ENVIRONMENT.

You genetically inherit certain physical, psychological and emotional qualities.

You also acquire and absorb qualities from your parents, friends, family, school, culture, media and religion.

All these qualities shape a sense of identity; who you believe you are.

Rigid beliefs and identity cast you in stone; blocking the flow of life force.

Rigid beliefs and identity also create 'us and them' perspectives, comparisons and judgements.

What would happen if you quit taking 'yourself' so seriously, and instead flowed as pure life force?

What if you understood that 'I' is an eternal witness, an observer of all the infinite qualities of life?

What if you walked through life observing and thinking 'It is what it is'?

How much inner peace and stillness would arise?

Right now, order my book I Am.

Stephen Shaw

DIVINE LOVERS

embrace

POSITIVITY and GRATITUDE

and let go

NEGATIVITY and COMPLAINING

When you look at the sky, you see rain clouds and sunshine.

No one is asking you to ignore the rain clouds.

Instead, you mindfully observe them.

You acknowledge their presence.

Then you settle your gaze on sunny light-blue sky.

Is it healthier to stare and brood at the cold rain?

Or to absorb and celebrate the gorgeous sun?

Is it useful to engage in negative gossip or supportive dialogue?

Is it beneficial to dwell on struggles and hardships or to focus on successes and milestones?

Is it helpful to recall past hurts or to make space for a potential beautiful future?

Are you easily pulled into drama or do you refuse to play that game?

If you sow seeds of negativity, you slowly create a rotten tree.

If you sow seeds of positivity, you steadily grow a luscious tree.

Positivity is partly a chosen attitude.

And partly a matter of perspective.

Here's a crucial word:

ENOUGH.

I am enough.

I have enough.

Many people focus on *scarcity*.

I am not good enough.

I do not have enough.

We naively believe that *abundance* is the answer.

I need to be more attractive, strong, skilful, wealthy.

On the contrary. Abundance is not the answer.

Abundance is not the opposite of scarcity.

Focusing on abundance means you are never satisfied.

I want more, more, more. I need more, more, more.

The answer is simply:

ENOUGH.

I am enough.

I have enough.

That is your mantra.

Your new viewpoint.

Your sacred chant.

Your new belief.

I am enough.

I have enough.

And along with that comes

GRATITUDE.

The holy elixir of serenity and peace.

No one is telling you not to strive for your dreams.

Nor to pursue your wishes and fantasies.

Yet …

Halt often …

Pause and breathe …

Notice the flowers …

Sense the love in your life …

Immerse in the precious moment …

Give thanks and heartfelt appreciation

For all you have

And all you are.

Celebrate.

Feel joy.

I am enough.

I have enough.

And remember,

Scarcity and Greed are not your friends.

Gratitude and Joy are your angels of Light.

Welcome them with open arms.

Stephen Shaw

DIVINE LOVERS

embrace

CURIOSITY and OPEN-MINDEDNESS

and let go

COMPARISON and JUDGEMENT

It is really simple.

Torment your mind with comparison and judgement.

Or know peace by acceptance of infinite differences.

May I introduce

Another mantra.

Say it often.

Absorb it.

It is what it is.

Or, if you prefer,

I am enough.

I have enough.

You are enough.

How does that feel?

An attitude of curiosity is a panacea for judgement.

Or even better …

An attitude of compassionate curiosity.

Or how about …

Heartfelt open-mindedness?

Those are like beautiful clothes.

Try them on and feel the sumptuousness.

The ethereal silky softness.

The stillness.

The peace.

Stephen Shaw

DIVINE LOVERS

embrace

MINDFULNESS and PRESENCE

and let go

DISTRACTIONS and MONKEY-MIND

Here Now.

This present moment.

This delightful event of Existence.

It really is

All happening

Here Now.

Did you miss it?

Were you present?

Or were you captivated by the past?

Entranced by edited-memory nostalgia *(not what it used to be)*.

Beguiled by could-have, should-have beens.

Mesmerised by wistful daydreams.

Anything to escape.

To be distracted.

Instead, try to

Feel your feet on the ground,

Breathe deeply, consciously,

Sense a delicate breeze,

Move your tongue,

Touch your nose,

Smell a flower,

Slowly gaze

Everywhere.

What are you seeing?

Sense-feeling?

Touching?

Scenting?

Hearing?

Tasting?

How alive is your body?

Notice the inner sensations.

Relax your shoulders.

Breathe deeply.

What's occurring in your mind?

Observe your thoughts.

Are they busy?

Where do they arise?

Where are they going?

Is there space between your thoughts?

Hmmm … How very interesting …

Music comprises notes and pauses.

Are you aware of the pauses?

Do you witness them?

Stillness lives there.

In this moment.

Here Now.

EMOTION

Stephen Shaw

DIVINE LOVERS

embrace

NEED FULFILMENT

and let go

LACK OF MEANING

Here is a tantalising secret.

A powerful key to your happiness.

Something to deeply ponder and absorb.

How often do you say "Life is meaningless"?

You posit that you are asking a metaphysical question.

If that is truly the case, the answer is:

THERE IS NO MEANING TO LIFE.

Nothing outside you.

Nothing beyond you.

Existence is a blank canvas.

A space of quantum possibilities.

YOU create reality and meaning.

YOU paint the blank canvas.

Read the book I Am by Stephen Shaw.

Then you will have esoteric understanding.

However ...

Mostly when you say "Life is meaningless"

What you are actually expressing is

"My life is unfulfilled and empty."

Read that again. Digest. Absorb.

More specifically, you are saying

"My emotional needs are unfulfilled."

Contemplate that truth deeply.

When your emotional needs are fulfilled,

You don't complain about existence or

Seek esoteric truths or meaning

Because you are **fulfilled,**

peaceful and **joyous!**

Aha. Riiiiiiight …

Stephen Shaw

DIVINE LOVERS

embrace

SELF-AWARENESS

and let go

SHADOWS

Backtrack briefly.

Your 'self' is a bouquet of transient, impermanent qualities.

A kind of temporary illusion that you take far too seriously.

Your 'Self' is eternal, underlying, permanent energy.

The Self is the Life Force, the Source, the Light.

That Light is in everyone and everything.

The Source is like a huge brilliant Diamond.

There is one Diamond with infinite facets.

Each facet is a reflection of the Source.

Every 'individual Self' is a facet.

Now, pay close attention …

DIVINE LOVERS embrace Self-awareness.

Hence, they concede that their true nature is God.

Or ultimate Life Force or the Source or the Light.

This cultivates a peace that surpasses understanding.

DIVINE LOVERS also embrace self-awareness.

Hence, they admit that their Earthly self is an illusion.

This generates wondrous laughter and merriment.

And the capability to play with illusion.

So … let's play and dance …

It's called Maya dialogue:

By yourself at a mirror.

Or with a close friend.

Simply ask a direct question to your self,

Or the close friend will ask your self:

"Please may I speak to the shadow."

Then answer immediately,

Without thinking.

Allow the shadow a voice.

Reveal your deepest thoughts.

Your hidden desires.

Your darkest truths.

No judgements.

No boundaries.

No barriers.

Bring all shadows into the light.

Own the shadows.

Accept the shadows.

Integrate the shadows.

Discover the entire self.

What are the consequences?

If you use compassionate curiosity,

And heartfelt open-mindedness,

There will be sighs of relief,

And reduction of anxiety,

Sense of wholeness,

Deepening peace,

Tears and joy.

DIVINE LOVERS

embrace

SELF-ACCEPTANCE

and let go

SHAME

Here is an intriguing secret.

A profound key to your happiness.

Something to deeply ponder and absorb.

The difference between GUILT and SHAME.

A colossal chasmic difference!

Guilt: I *did* something bad.

Guilt is healthy.

Shame: I *am* bad.

Shame is destructive.

Shame is a terrible lie.

Shame is a form of control.

Never accept shame. Ever.

Shame is an insidious poison.

When it arises, apply the antidote:

Self-empathy

Self-acceptance

Self-compassion

Soothing self-talk.

Hearing the rebound.

Sensing your resistance.

What if you feel different to most people?

Everyone has shadows, quirks and idiosyncrasies.

Those very terms are based on comparisons and judgements.

Comparisons and judgements are foisted on you from the outside.

From parents, friends, family, school, culture, media and religion.

You are indoctrinated and absorb it as an internal 'reality'.

None of it is natural. None of it is innate. None of it is real.

Your true nature is pure, free, loving consciousness.

All the self-qualities are an illusion that you accept.

Self-awareness reminds you that

YOU alone create your reality.

Choose something different.

Self-empathy

Self-acceptance

Self-compassion

Soothing self-talk.

It's all DIVINE LOVE.

Stephen Shaw

DIVINE LOVERS

embrace

AUTHENTICITY and BOUNDARIES

and let go

OTHER PEOPLE'S OPINIONS

Wow! Are you ready for this?

In a world so influential,

Full of sticky social webs,

Can you be truly free?

Do you dare to be yourself?

DIVINE LOVERS are self-aware and self-accepting.

The next step is to express all of you.

AUTHENTIC

Open

Real

Raw.

Put aside what other people think.

Put aside all the fears and anxieties.

Put aside comparison and judgement.

Remember ...

I AM ENOUGH.

In a world that highlights

Extraordinary achievements

Cool, awesome lifestyles

Trending fashions

Attractiveness,

You forget sometimes

THAT WE ARE ALL ORDINARY.

You don't have to hide yourself.

How about …

Sharing your truest deepest story.

Being seen and known.

Expressing your truth.

Living authentically.

Not everyone has to like your self.

Everyone has preferences, likes and dislikes.

If your qualities don't resonate with their qualities

Then you just don't dance together.

And that's alright.

It's all fine.

DIVINE LOVERS have healthy BOUNDARIES.

Being authentic does not mean you share all of you with everyone.

You choose with whom to share your various qualities.

You respect other people's boundaries too.

What is appropriate to share?

How much trust is there?

Is it a close friend?

Acquaintance?

Take a pause.

Contemplate.

Sense-feel.

Practice.

Flex your boundaries.

Sometimes say "No."

And sometimes be

Raw

Real

Open.

There are infinite differences.

And it's all kind of wonderful.

Skin colour, ethnicity, gender, sexual orientation.

Gregarious extrovert, introspective loner.

Artistic, musical, academic, sporty.

Outdoors adventurer, homebody.

Whatever-dude, sensitive soul.

It's all beautiful.

It's all flowing

Life Force.

Ooooooh ...

What about the sensitive types?

Sensitivity is usually genetic.

It has a physical basis.

An enhanced nervous system.

It makes you sensitive to stimuli.

Both environmental (external to you)

And within (bodily sensations).

Hence, you are sensitive to light, sound, touch, taste, scent.

And you are sensitive to changes in your body feelings.

And you are sensitive to moods and energy in people.

You often process information more deeply.

Including body language and micro-cues.

Making you appear very intuitive.

Such attentiveness can be tiring.

Requiring recharging in solitude.

And regular sessions of quiet-time.

Physical sensitivity is *not* introversion.

Introversion is a psychological trait.

Yes, the world comprises an intriguing array of people.

YOU choose the appropriate level of **authenticity**.

YOU choose the level and types of **boundaries**.

YOU decide with whom you will interact.

And to what degree and how much.

Listen to this nonchalant vibration:

Hand In My Pocket by Alanis Morissette:

'What it all comes down to, is that

'Everything's gonna be quite alright

'Everything's gonna be fine, fine, fine.'

The dance is in your hands.

Or perhaps in your feet.

Cue the music …

DIVINE LOVERS

embrace

BEING VULNERABLE

and let go

FEAR OF REJECTION

Authenticity requires vulnerability.

It feels like a risk of being harmed.

Yet, how can you be harmed?

Because someone doesn't like you?

Because your qualities don't resonate with theirs?

Everyone has preferences, likes and dislikes.

Their preferences have nothing to do with you.

Vulnerability may seem like a weakness.

To whom exactly? And why?

Is it weak to shine your light?

To show up and be seen?

To express who you are?

Explore these yummylicious secrets:

Deep connections require authenticity.

True intimacy requires vulnerability.

Heartfelt love requires *shields down*.

Chant your sacred mantra:

I AM ENOUGH.

No need for vigilance.

No need for anxiety.

No need for fear.

Say it softly.

Shout it loud.

I AM ENOUGH.

Have the courage

To share your

Thoughts

Feelings

Desires

Needs

Self.

Learn whom you can trust.

Adopt flexible boundaries.

Dance appropriately.

Be astute and flow.

Be yourself.

Here comes love …

Love is uncertain and risky.

Life is impermanence and change.

There are no guaranteed outcomes.

Would you rather be alone and safe?

Or expose yourself to exquisiliciousness?

Not knowing about next week or next year.

Knowing fulfilment in this precious moment,

And savouring bliss and joy in the Here Now.

Alright … let's turn around the whole concept.

Have you considered what *you* are offering?

Did you create a sacred space for intimacy?

A trusting place to listen to your partner?

To allow their authenticity?

To nurture their vulnerability?

Sometimes our own fear of vulnerability

Means we …

Unconsciously …

Shut down our partner's vulnerability!

If you react with disappointment or disgust,

You can be sure your partner will

No longer open up to you.

Instead they will be

Cautious

Secretive

Shielded

Defensive

Disconnected.

And your romantic relationship

(or friendship or family situation)

Will feel empty, alone, unfulfilled.

Thus, it is your responsibility

To not only risk and share,

To not only be vulnerable,

But to consciously and intentionally

Create and foster a receptive energy,

A compassionately curious attitude,

A loving-kind sacred space,

For reciprocal and flowing

Authenticity and vulnerability.

It's the next level of relationship.

Deep, raw, authentic, vulnerable.

The sacredness of Divine Love.

DIVINE LOVERS

embrace

DEEP CONNECTIONS

and let go

WALKING ALONE IN LIFE

Cast your mind back.

Do you recall this idea?

Mostly when you say "Life is meaningless"

What you are actually expressing is

"My life is unfulfilled and empty."

More specifically, you are saying

"My emotional needs are unfulfilled."

Contemplate these sage and heartfelt truths:

We are primed for deep personal connections.

We are innately programmed for love and belonging.

Connections infuse you with fulfilment, peace and joy.

When you find yourself saying "Life is meaningless"

Or "Life is pointless" or "Life is empty",

Replace that phrase immediately with

"Am I deeply connected to MYSELF and OTHERS?"

You understand self-awareness, self-acceptance, authenticity.

Now let's advance you into fulfilling relationships.

What are the requirements for deep connections?

Absolutely no surprise ... *you know!*

Self-awareness

Self-acceptance

Authenticity

Vulnerability

Boundaries.

Acquaintances are great.

Compatriots are wonderful.

Here are noteworthy questions:

How many confidants do you have?

Who will listen to your anxieties and fears?

Who will help you face a huge challenge?

Who will heed your hopes and dreams?

Have you invested in deep friendships?

Have you nurtured vulnerability in relationships?

If you still doubt the significance of connections,

Ponder this thought-provoking information:

Depression and anxiety are tightly entangled.

The primary cause of both is **disconnection**.

Disconnection from your purpose and passions.

Right now, order my book Heart Song.

Disconnection from deep relationships.

Right now, order my book They Walk Among Us.

Right now, order my book The Other Side.

Disconnection from love and sexuality.

Right now, order my book The Sorcerer.

Right now, order my book The Tribe.

Disconnection from divine loving.

(You're reading this book now.)

And finally, a huge one ...

Disconnection arising from childhood trauma.

(Details in the next chapter.)

As a last thought-pointer ...

You know yourself best.

You know what you need.

Deep connections and alone time.

Find the balance of solitude and intimacy.

Whichever way brings you deepest fulfilment.

DIVINE LOVERS

embrace

HEALTHY RELATIONSHIPS

and let go

DYSFUNCTIONAL STYLES

Ouch!

Who wants to hear the word 'dysfunction'?

Yet, we've all chosen friends and lovers

Using unconscious or childhood strategies

That simply no longer benefit us as adults.

Sadly, the number one dysfunction arises

From childhood abuse and or neglect.

This is possibly the most important lesson.

Perhaps you will recognise your style.

This is a well-researched psychological theory:

RELATIONSHIP ATTACHMENTS *(John Bowlby)*

It all starts with the primary caretaker (parent).

The primary caretaker should be providing:

Proximity

Presence, loving-kindness.

Secure Base

Safety, allowing exploration.

Unfortunately, some parents provided:

Abuse, neglect and or abandonment.

Caretaking creates an attachment style in the child.

This attachment style is *very* deeply engrained.

You carry your style into adult relationships.

SECURE attachment style

This results from healthy parenting. Caretaker was present, attentive, loving, kind, and provided a sense of security. Such children are *interdependent, feel good about themselves and others;* believe they are worthy of love; and easily regulate their emotions. They will comfortably pursue healthy relationships later in life.

ANXIOUS attachment style

This results from unhealthy parenting. Caretaker was unavailable and or a scaremonger about the outside world. The child is anxious, needing attachment to the caretaker, and less likely to explore the outside world. The child is *dependent, insecure about own worth but feels good about others.* The child often escapes into spirituality; seeking certainty and security from powerful supernatural beings.

AVOIDANT-DISMISSIVE attachment style

This results from unhealthy parenting. Caretaker was neglectful and or threatening. The child consequently avoids closeness and intimacy, feels empty and alone, suppresses feelings, has strong defences, and may be prone to dissociation. The child is *independent, feels good about themselves but does not trust others;* tends to be vigilant for environmental threats. The child often escapes into intellectualism and or spirituality; seeking love and meaning from benevolent supernatural beings; and tends to be disconnected from own body and or the Earth.

AVOIDANT-FEARFUL attachment style

This results from unhealthy parenting. Caretaker was very neglectful and or abusive. The child consequently avoids closeness and intimacy, feels empty and alone, has strong defences, and may be prone to shyness, dissociation, depression and anxiety. The child has poor emotion-regulation. The child is *independent, insecure about own worth and does not trust others.* The child often escapes into intellectualism and or spirituality; seeking love and approval and meaning from benevolent supernatural beings; and tends to be disconnected from own body and or the Earth.

Did you manage to find your style?

We survive by adapting to our environment.

Your style was a successful coping response as a child.

Which gradually crystallised into rigid beliefs and identity.

Unfortunately, as an adult this does not always benefit you.

If you carry an *insecure attachment style (anxious or avoidant)* into a romantic relationship, and or attract a partner with an *insecure attachment style,* you will experience serious challenges and struggles.

DIVINE LOVERS embrace **healthy relationships** and let go dysfunctional styles.

How do you do that?

What are the tools?

Therapy

Presence

Curiosity

Compassion

Mindfulness

Self-awareness

Self-acceptance

Authenticity

Vulnerability

Boundaries

Sense your body

Inhabit your body

Feel your emotions

Regulate your emotions

Seek deep connections

Engage in relationships

Surrender to intimacy

Inhabit beautiful Earth

Create heaven on Earth.

Stephen Shaw

DIVINE LOVERS

embrace

INTIMACY

and let go

DETACHMENT

You've come this far …

Opened your mind.

Shifted your beliefs.

Refined your identity.

Established trust and faith.

Committed to authenticity.

Dedicated to vulnerability.

Seeking deep connections.

It's time to get INTIMATE

With a romantic partner,

Psychologically

Emotionally

Physically

Sensually

Sexually.

This is the greatest risk in relationships.

And brings the greatest fulfilment and joy.

Radical truth and transparency.

Compassionate curiosity.

Ardent loving-kindness.

Flexible boundaries.

Stripped to the core.

Deep engagement.

Acceptance.

Eye-gazing.

Adventure.

Generosity.

Creativity.

Surrender.

Listening.

Presence.

Pleasure.

Freedom.

Novelty.

Nesting.

Respect.

Savour.

Dance.

Peace.

Play.

Fun.

Joy.

SPIRIT

Stephen Shaw

DIVINE LOVERS

embrace

FORGIVENESS

and let go

ANGER

There is genuine harm.

There is also fragile ego.

There is your fixed beliefs.

There is your rigid identity.

Be careful of holding onto anger for the wrong reason.

As the Buddha said:

'Holding onto anger is like grasping a hot coal.'

Yes, it's only burning you.

DIVINE LOVERS focus on need fulfilment.

You discuss your needs with your partner

Or friends or family or work colleagues.

This requires ... again, no surprises:

Mindfulness

Self-awareness

Self-acceptance

Authenticity

Vulnerability

Boundaries.

When you do not get your needs met,

You formulate a new strategy.

Sometimes you accept reality.

Here is another mantra:

Strategize

then

Surrender

and

Flow.

Here is a very useful skill to acquire.

And it rightfully deserves an entire book:

Nonviolent Communication by Marshall Rosenberg

Read it. Absorb it. Practice the techniques.

You are striving to feel good.

Forgiveness creates release.

Forgiveness creates space.

Forgiveness creates peace.

It sets your spirit free.

To love divinely.

Stephen Shaw

DIVINE LOVERS

embrace

LOVING-KINDNESS

and let go

INDIFFERENCE

The opposite of loving-kindness is not meanness or cruelty.

A healthy person would very soon leave such a relationship.

No, the opposite of loving-kindness is *indifference*.

Being in a relationship that constantly

Leaves you hanging,

Wanting more,

Unfulfilled,

Ignored,

Alone.

Or feeling unnoticed and invisible in life.

Indifference is a psycho-emotional killer.

Loving-kindness is soulful presence.

From my book The Sorcerer:

Rinpoche shows his upturned palm.

"Compassion, which is the vital attitude and energy."

He shows his other upturned palm.

"Loving-kindness, which is the crucial action and doing."

He slaps his palms together, with dramatic effect.

"Neither one by itself. Both aspects are essential."

The lyrics of *Bring Me To Life* by Evanescence:

'How can you see into my eyes, like open doors

'Leading you down into my core

'Where I've become so numb

'Without a soul

'My spirit's sleeping somewhere cold

'Until you find it there and lead it back

'Home

'Wake me up, wake me up inside.'

That's how many of us feel in life

And in romantic relationships.

The antidote to emptiness?

From my book They Walk Among Us:

'This exquisite union of the hearts … I think it is what we are all seeking. Perhaps love in all its forms is the one true antidote to the strange, struggling emptiness of existence.'

Let's sum it up in two words.

The beatific antidote is **Divine Love**.

DIVINE LOVERS embrace **loving-kindness**.

You meditate on loving-kindness.

You breathe loving-kindness.

You invite loving-kindness.

You share loving-kindness.

You give loving-kindness.

You know it starts

With you

Here

Now.

Mindfulness and presence.

Intense open-heartedness.

Forging deep connections.

Investing in relationships.

Following the guidelines.

Practicing the techniques.

Being a DIVINE LOVER.

As you flow love divinely

In your romantic relationship,

Gently discuss your needs with your partner.

Consider giving her my book DIVINE LOVE.

Or insouciantly leaving it on his bedside table.

Who knows ...

One day you may be ready for **Tantra**.

Tantra is the greatest relationship skill.

Tantra embodies and embraces:

Intense open-heartedness.

Chakras energy magick.

Soulful connectedness.

Playful sensuality.

Yummy sexuality.

OMG orgasms.

Kundalini.

It's exquisilicious Divine Love!

Right now, order my book The Tribe.

Right now, order my book Heart Song.

Right now, order my book The Sorcerer.

Right now, order my book They Walk Among Us.

Those books contain Tantric and relationship skills.

Once you've read them, you may seek a teacher.

Someone with honesty, integrity and kindness.

You'll work within your comfort parameters.

You'll let yourself surrender and flow too.

A gorgeous, fulfilling relationship awaits!

It's time to become a DIVINE LOVER.

And ultimately a DIVINE TANTRIKA.

DIVINE LOVERS

embrace

GENEROSITY

and let go

GREED

Let's make a clear distinction:

Selfishness is healthy.

Greed is harmful.

DIVINE LOVERS are self-aware and self-accepting.

DIVINE LOVERS strive for need fulfilment.

That's beautiful and necessary.

No one is asking you to sacrifice yourself

Or give up your needs, desires and dreams.

DIVINE LOVERS balance own and others' needs.

DIVINE LOVERS practice loving-kindness.

DIVINE LOVERS practice generosity.

Greed harms

Me and you,

Other people,

Other tribes,

Other nations,

Pristine nature,

Our precious Earth.

Greed takes and steals.

Greed says: 'I want more, more, more!'

Greed says: 'Me, Me, Me, Me, Me.'

Generosity heals

Me and you,

Other people,

Other tribes,

Other nations,

Pristine nature,

Our precious Earth.

Generosity is loving and kind.

Generosity says: 'Let's share.'

Generosity says: 'It's about us.'

Generosity makes you feel good.

Generosity connects you to others.

Generosity alleviates depression.

Generosity has no strings attached.

Generosity does not expect a return.

Generosity is a spiritual gift.

It may be time or energy,

products or resources.

Whatever fulfils needs.

It's all DIVINE LOVE.

DIVINE LOVERS

embrace

LEGACY

and let go

INSULARITY

From my book Heart Song:

'Always remember your legacy.

'What have you inherited?

'What are you giving to the world?

'What will you leave behind when you are gone?'

Legacy is a natural extension of generosity.

Pay heed to the words of Maya Angelou:

'Your legacy is every life you've touched.'

Ponder that for a while.

Every day in every way,

You are leaving a legacy.

Every interaction counts.

Every action matters.

Supporting an orphanage,

Driving an electric car,

Donating to a charity,

Mentoring a teenager,

Smiling at a stranger,

Nurturing a friend,

Words of kindness,

Helping a family,

Riding a bicycle,

Planting a tree,

Deep listening,

Going green,

Confidante,

Teaching.

Mahatma Gandhi said:

'You must be the change you want to see in the world.'

Stephen Shaw is saying:

'Change your own world into Divine Love.

'Become an accomplished Divine Lover.

'Then shine the Light of Divine Love.

'Upon the rest of the world.'

Divine Love

Is

All

That

Matters.

Stephen Shaw

DIVINE LOVERS

embrace

AWAKENING

and let go

IGNORANCE

Right now, order my book The Fractal Key.

Right now, order my book Reflections.

Right now, order my book Star Child.

Right now, order my book I Am.

Right now, order my book 5D.

To complete the Spirit section, let's explore

AWAKENING and ULTIMATE AWARENESS.

So ... here we are ...

Awakening, altered states and higher levels of consciousness have been covered in many of my books (see list above).

What I'm interested in sharing is what I call

POST-AWAKENING.

To dispel the myths and confusion of the ultimate journey.

Why Journey? Why Seek?

This may be hard to hear. Keep an open mind.

The majority of people seek the mysterious Beyond and ethereal Beings for one simple reason: To escape this 'terrible' reality. This may result from a tough childhood or insecure attachment style (including anxiety, suppressed feelings, body dissociation, disconnection from other people) or observing the 'insanity' on our planet (corrupt politicians, misogyny, racism, destruction of forests and animals, and so on).

In that case, Seeking is not a solution.

Divine Love is the solution.

Therapy is a solution.

GOYA is a solution
(get off your ass).

For example:

Speak with your vote.

Improve your carbon footprint.

Join ethical movements for change.

Participate in protests and marches.

Share your ideas on social media.

Help the deprived and destitute.

Support conservation charities.

Consider your legacy.

Do something good!

If you are already living with your feet planted firmly on planet Earth, and you have adopted the principles of Divine Love, and worked through any psycho-emotional issues, AND you wish to seek the highest dimensions of consciousness and savour the magick that lies beyond this realm ...

Well, that's another matter entirely.

I call such people True Seekers.

True Seeking

Everything I know and have experienced is expounded in my spiritual mystical books. I should mention that my books are deeply layered and sprinkled with hidden gems. So keep your mind and eyes open. Find all my books at my website: www.i-am-stephen-shaw.com

Here is an idea that will serve you well ...

Seeking is based on desire. It is *mind* that grasps.

Yet the very thing that seeks and grasps is the barrier.

Imagine a drop of water in the ocean.

All that separates the drop from the ocean

Is a flimsy, delicate (illusory) barrier.

Ponder the flimsy barrier *seeking* that which

SURROUNDS IT

And is

INSIDE IT.

Is there anything to grasp or attain?

The drop and ocean are the same.

The drop already is the ocean!

The harder the mind seeks,

The more it reinforces itself,

And the barrier remains.

Awakening is *not about*

Seeking

Chasing

Grasping

Attaining

Acquiring

Achieving

Controlling

Becoming

Evolving

Growing.

La Petite Mort

(French, 'the little death')

Awakening is *about*

Surrendering

Witnessing

Observing

Letting go

Lessening

Flowing

Losing.

The barrier needs to *diminish*

So the ocean flows into the drop.

Whatever techniques you choose,

Whichever catalysts you employ,

From mindfulness to meditation

To the mystical fractal keys,

It is all about letting go.

Many tiny ego deaths.

Less of you / self.

Unveiling Self.

The Blue Butterfly

There once was a young woman

Who wore a turquoise t-shirt

With the words True Seeker

Emblazoned sensationally.

A gorgeous, radiant blue butterfly

Always sat on the tip of her nose.

Yet, she spent every waking hour

Searching through the forests,

Seeking, chasing, grasping

For an elusive, radiant

Blue butterfly.

The Drop Becomes The Ocean

If you experience Ultimate Consciousness

And permanently merge into the Source

(the drop merges completely with the ocean),

You cease to 'exist' in this realm / reality.

You are the Unmanifested Consciousness.

You are the Source. You are the Light.

There is no drop; only the vast ocean.

It is doubtful that this is your wish.

Interestingly, you have a choice.

Jay's wisdom *(from my book I Am):*

From where I am sitting, you have a few choices: You exit this reality and stay in the Light; you surf through different realities enjoying the great Dance of Life; or you stay in this reality and make a difference on this planet. These are the choices for every enlightened being.

Post-Awakening

It's no wonder I never hear this discussed.

There are few awakened beings on Earth.

You'll *know* when you're awakened.

You'll *know* when I AM happens!

It's an *experience.*

It's an *event.*

What happens after awakening?

You are ecstatic and blissed out,

Lost, confused and disoriented,

Barely able to function on Earth.

This may continue for days,

Or weeks or even months.

Then you do the shopping,

Drive the kids to school,

Read bedtime stories,

Make breakfast,

Do the laundry,

Mow the lawn,

Go to work.

Earthly life continues.

You will find yourself

Living, breathing, working,

In various states of consciousness.

Ram Dass said:

'If you think you're enlightened, go spend a week with your family.'

Similar sentiments may arise

When standing in a long queue,

Receiving unjust treatment,

Needing morning coffee,

Craving dark chocolate.

You have the idea.

Here's the tingle.

After awakening,

When you find yourself

In what *you* call

'lower states of consciousness',

You start to feel frustrated

And disappointed

And concerned.

Questions circulate quietly.

Where is the enlightenment?

Where did the I AM disappear?

Where is Ultimate Consciousness?

Perhaps the monkey-mind reappears.

And the seeking-grasping begins again.

Forever chasing that Supreme Sweetness.

How Many Gears Do You Need?

If you were stuck in I AM consciousness,

What Earthly good would you be?

How would you go to work?

How would you feed your children?

How would you function effectively?

You may as well live in a remote cave.

And spend the rest of your life there.

Contemplate this ...

When you drive your car

Or bicycle *(if green-focused)*,

How many gears do you need?

Imagine driving a car constantly

In first gear

Or fifth gear.

How successful would you be?

Awakening is touching fifth gear.

It will always be present in you.

Tantric chakra sex is fourth gear.

Deep meditation is third gear.

Grocery shopping is second.

Studying is first gear.

(more or less)

Post-awakening means you flow

Through various states of consciousness,

And employ levels of consciousness,

Depending on the situation,

Contingent on the context.

You accept and know that

You are driving a car

With five gears.

And it is necessary

To *use all five gears*

To function optimally.

Judgement need not arise.

Nor any self-deprecation.

Instead, you simply flow

In a high-functional way.

Smoothly operating as a

Multi-dimensional

Awakened

Being.

Ultimate Freedom

Neti-neti is a Sanskrit expression

Which means 'not this, not that'

Or 'neither this, nor that'.

The phrase is found in

The Upanishads and
(Supreme Knowledge)

The Avadhuta Gita
(Song Of The Free).

And this is your final lesson.

Truly free consciousness

That

FEELS GOOD

And

OPERATES EFFECTIVELY

Is neither stuck in Ultimate Consciousness

Nor stuck in mundane Earthly consciousness;

Is neither stuck in the non-dual perspective

Nor stuck in the dualistic perspective;

Is neither grasping desperately

Nor clinging hopefully

To any particular

Way of being.

Awaken.

Transcend.

Then go beyond.

Witness

Move

Flow

Love

Live

Be.

Then, my dear

DIVINE LOVER,

You are truly **free.**

And overflowing with

Fulfilment, peace and joy.

Stephen Shaw's Books

Visit the website: www.i-am-stephen-shaw.com

I Am contains spiritual and mystical teachings from enlightened masters that point the way to love, peace, bliss, freedom and spiritual awakening.

Heart Song takes you on a mystical adventure into creating your reality and manifesting your dreams, and reveals the secrets to attaining a fulfilled and joyful life.

They Walk Among Us is a love story spanning two realities. Explore the mystery of the angels. Discover the secrets of Love Whispering.

The Other Side explores the most fundamental question in each reality. What happens when the physical body dies? Where do you go? Expand your awareness. Journey deep into the Mystery.

Reflections offers mystical words for guidance, meditation and contemplation. Open the book anywhere and unwrap your daily inspiration.

5D is the Fifth Dimension. Discover ethereal doorways hidden in the fabric of space-time. Seek the advanced mystical teachings.

Star Child offers an exciting glimpse into the future on earth. The return of the gods and the advanced mystical teachings. And the ultimate battle of light versus darkness.

The Tribe expounds the joyful creation of new Earth. What happened after the legendary battle of Machu Picchu? What is Christ consciousness? What is Ecstatic Tantra?

The Fractal Key reveals the secrets of the shamans. This handbook for psychonauts discloses the techniques and practices used in psychedelic healing and transcendent journeys.

Stephen Shaw's Books

Atlantis illuminates the Star Beings and Earth's Ancient History. A magical history ingrained in your deepest consciousness, in your myths and mysteries. Discover the secret teachings of the star beings.

The Sorcerer is a journey into Magick, Power and Mysticism. Discover the Twelve Auspicious Symbols. Explore the paths of Awareness, Love and Tantra. Absorb the sacred teachings and mantras of the lamas.

Divine Love is a guide on how to truly live. It's about authenticity, intimacy and freedom. It's about discovering and accepting your true nature. Bringing profound, overwhelming Love into your precious existence. Embracing OMGorgeous exquisilicious feelings of fulfilment, peace and joy. Creating a slice of heaven on Earth.

CPSIA information can be obtained
at www.ICGtesting.com
Printed in the USA
LVHW080838291119
638506LV00004B/323/P